COME MIME WITH ME

A Guide to Preparing Scriptural Dramas for Children

By Gail Kelley
with Carol Hershberger
Illustrations by Carol Hershberger

 Resource Publications, Inc.
160 E. Virginia St. No. 290
San Jose, CA 95112

Editorial Director: Kenneth Guentert
Illustrations: Carol Hershberger
Design: Christine Benjamin, Kenneth Guentert
Production Artists: Geoff Rogers, Ron Niewald

ISBN 0-89390-089-3
Library of Congress Catalog Number 86-62621
Printed and Bound in the United States 5 4 3 2 1

Text and artwork copyright © 1987 by Gail Kelley and Carol Hershberger. All rights reserved. Purchase of book includes the right to reproduce illustrations and text for classroom purposes only. For reprint permission, write to Reprint Department, Resource Publications, Inc., 160 E. Virginia St. No. 290, San Jose, CA 95112.

TABLE OF CONTENTS

ACKNOWLEDGEMENTS iv
DEDICATION vii
PURPOSE viii
PREFACE x
THE SIMPLER THE BETTER xii
LET'S PUT A DRAMA TOGETHER 1
DRAMAS
    1. SPREAD THE WORD 9
    2. ME USEFUL OR (A CACTUS WHO FOUND HIS PLACE) .. 17
    3. C.T., J.C. AND ME 25
    4. THE ONE GREAT HOLY SPIRIT 33
    5. THEY SHARED SOMETHING TOGETHER 41
    6. INVITE THEM IN 47
    7. MORE TIMES THAN YOU CAN COUNT 55
    8. STRAIGHT BUT NARROW 63
    9. SURPRISED 71
    10. PROOF OF THE PUDDING 77
I LIKED YOUR DRAMAS BECAUSE 81
JUST A REMINDER 83
CRITIQUE SHEET 84
QUIET THOUGHTS 86
NOTES 90

ACKNOWLEDGEMENTS

We wish to express many thanks to the children of St. Ann's School, Ridgecrest, CA., and to its Pastor, Monsignor Kevin Cleary; Principal, Dan Clark and to all the teaching staff. Your support has been so generous and loving. We also thank Bill and Mary Britton of Heritage Productions, of Ridgecrest, CA., and Fred Shaughnessy who were instrumental in producing a videotape for us. Many thanks to Pius X Catholic School in Norfolk, VA, and in particular its principal, Sr. Francis John, I.H.M., for allowing us to take snapshots of her students for *Come Mime With Me*. Personal thanks go to Mike Inman for his knowledge of legal matters and to Carla Schneider and Ruby Tillie of Holy Family Parish in Virginia Beach, VA, for their help in the duplicating and sorting department.

Much gratitude goes to those who were there for us in the final stages of publication: Charles Hibbs, Cox High School, Virginia Beach, VA, for poster art work; Mary Almaguer, Director of Religious Education for Naval Air Station, Key West, FL; Sr. Elaine McCarron, S.C.N., Minister of Religious Education, Holy Spirit Catholic Church, Virginia Beach, VA; Suzanne Hall, SND deN, Executive Director, Special Education Department of National Catholic Education Association, Washington, D.C.; Sr. Rita Baum, S.S.J., Director of the National Catholic Office For Persons With Disabilities, Washington, D.C.; Sr. Alverna Hollis, O.P., Director of the National Catholic Office For The Deaf, Washington, D.C.; Sr. Mary Ann Schmitz, S.M.P., loving friend and Principal of St. Patrick's School, Washington, IL; Dr. Henry H. Thompkins, Pastor, United Methodist Church, Ridgecrest, CA; Brother Louis De Thomasis, F.S.C., PhD, President, St. Mary's College, Winona, MI; Reverend Gerald Mahon, Rector, St. Mary's Seminary, Winona, MI; Brother Phillip Dougherty, C.F.X., Administrative Promoter of Justice, Diocese of Richmond, VA; Reverend Ronald A. Ruth, Pastor, Pius X Catholic Church, Norfolk, VA; and the Most Reverend Walter F. Sullivan D.D., Bishop, Diocese of Richmond, VA. For opening our eyes to the publishing merit of *Come Mime With Me,* many thanks and lots of warm fuzzies go to Darlene Pienta, M.A., Religious Education, Fordham University, NY, publishing consultant and dear beautiful friend. With love I thank my husband, Dave, for editing the final manuscript.

Thanks to Tabor Publishing, a division of DLM, Inc., Allen, TX 75002 USA for giving us permission to use exerpts from *The Seventh Trumpet* by Mark Link, S.J., Copyright © 1978 Tabor Publishing, Allen TX 75002.

Excerpts from the *New American Bible*, Copyright © 1970 by the Confraternity of Christian Doctrine, Washington, D.C. are used with permission of copyright owner. All rights reserved.

DEDICATION

Dear Father, Son and Holy Spirit,

To You we dedicate this endeavor to "make known your love and will for us all." It was really You that authored *Come Mime With Me*. We thank You for allowing us to be your instruments.

Please shower your many blessings upon all those who have guided us through so many experiences that have enables this book, your work, to be accomplished.

From Gail,

I dedicate *Come Mime With Me* to my husband David and four children; Leah, Jacqui, Sarah and Nicholas. By their love, understanding and compassion, I have grown to see my calling in an even deeper sense through authorship. Most especially I dedicate *Come Mime With Me* to all of God's children everywhere, no matter what their ages may be.

Thank you to all of my Cursillo grouping friends who have encouraged and prayed for the success of this writing. Carol and Darlene, I Love You! You have given me what thirteen years of schooling could never do, a sense of belief in myself. A special thanks to my natural father, Murray (Popso), Mary, my gentle mom, and dear friend and stepfather, LeRoy. You have all given me the roots necessary to keep on 'Keeping On.'

From Carol,

Very special thanks and blessings go to my husband John and son Eric. Their patience and enduring love as I struggled to learn the workings of the "Word Processor" make them deserving of Sainthood.

God showers so many gifts upon us. One of the most beautiful has been in knowing Gail Kelley. It has been a gift of friendship that I wish to savor for all eternity.

PURPOSE

Father Ken Roberts, celebrated speaker and noted author, made an important point that has colored our approach to teaching scripture. His premise is based on simplicity. People need to be able to walk away with a "one-liner" that will summarize the entire message. Without that "one-liner" people will be less equipped to relate God's Word to their daily lives.

Our desire is that scripture become easily accessible. This book will provide you with the elementary ideas needed to relate God's Word to everyday situations. It is *not* meant to be a collection of several mini-narrated dramas to employ carte-blanche. Instead it is to be a hands-on guide to developing your own simple (non-professional) dramas based on that one-liner message from scripture.

"Faith ... comes through hearing, and what is heard is the word of Christ" (Romans 10:17 NAB). With that in mind, we have preceded each drama with a pertinent scripture reading. Because we feel it is important to get across to the audience that our source, for the sake of validity, is the Bible, we ask that you physically use the Bible to read the scripture reference. We emphasize that need by not supplying you with the complete written scripture.

We use many different translations and paraphrases of Bibles, both Catholic and Protestant. Our reasoning is that all Bibles are valid and valuable to a vast array of personalities. "Different Strokes for Different Folks." All versions are adaptable to today's situations: King James, The Good News Bible or The Book.

It has been our goal from the beginning to develop a viable, tangible educational tool. To allow *Come Mime With Me* to speak for itself, we have added two essential aids to every drama; a concise drama overview and a reinforcing follow-up. As teachers, we have found the overview and follow-up a must. They make for quick and easy access to preparing and finishing each assigned drama. The information box at the top of the drama overview page is self explanatory. All of the vital statistics are capsulized in one clear-cut area. The follow-up becomes the recollection of the "one-liner" that will make the picture (drama) worth a thousand words.

It has become our purpose and goal to reach a wider audience. Sr. Rita Baum, S.S.J., Director of the National Office for Persons With Disabilities and Sr. Alverna Holis, O.P., Director of the National Catholic Office for The Deaf have encouraged us to broaden our perspective. Upon reviewing *Come Mime With Me,* both women envisioned angels jumping from the slab of marble, as Michelangelo might have. It was their opinion that our book could be a valuable tool for teaching scripture to those with any type of handicap. We shall be eternally grateful for their insight when we lacked it!

The principles behind *Come Mime With Me* allow it to be easily adapted for a variety of uses. These uses include monthly Cub Scout evenings, retreat planning, parenting, counseling, religious education of any faith and at work or anywhere a Christian message is the desired end product.

Through the use of simple mimed dramas, God's message will be easily understood and longlasting.

Enjoy!

PREFACE

MATTHEW 7:24-27

Jesus said: "Anyone who hears my words and puts them into practice is like the wise man who built his house on rock.

"When the rainy season set in, the torrents came and the winds blew and buffeted his house. It did not collapse; it had been solidly set on rock.

"Anyone who hears my words but does not put them into practice is like the foolish man who built his house on sandy ground.

"The rains fell, the torrents came, the winds blew and lashed against his house. It collapsed."

LUKE 6:47-49

Jesus said: "Any man who desires to come to me will hear my words and put them into practice...He may be likened to the man who, in building a house, dug deeply and laid the foundation on a rock.

"When the floods came the torrent rushed in on that house, but failed to shake it because of its solid foundation...

"Anyone who has heard my words but not put them into practice is like the man who built his house on the ground without any foundation.

"When the torrent rushed upon it, it immediately fell in."

Mark Link, author of *The Seventh Trumpet* writes, "Jesus made wide use of stories called parables. A parable is a simile drawn from life or nature, designed to arrest the hearer's attention and to prod the hearer's imagination ...

"Parables taught about God's kingdom by using simple comparisons familiar to all. They helped people move slowly but surely from the known to the unknown. Parables helped people to prod their imaginations and stretch their minds to embrace ideas and possibilities bigger than those to which they were normally accustomed.

"Finally, besides revealing the nature of God's kingdom and the messiah, parables revealed the status of peoples' hearts. Parables invited people to discover themselves as they really were: open or closed to the truth.

"Since a parable did not make it directly, it gave people the option of accepting or rejecting the deeper meaning to which it pointed ... Thus, parables acted as a kind of test to see if a person's heart was open or closed. Concerning people with closed hearts, Jesus remarked to his disciples:

"'They listen but do not hear or understand. Isaiah's prophecy is fulfilled in them which says ...'

"Sluggish indeed is this people's heart..."

"But blest are your eyes because they see and blest are your ears because they hear."
    Matthew 13:13-16

Using the parable of the man who built his house on a rock, Matthew 7:24-27 and Luke 6:47-49, Mark Link examines the same story told two different ways:

"Comparing these two versions, we notice slight but interesting variations. Some readers explain these variations, saying Jesus probably told the same parable to different groups on two different occasions."

"Others note that Matthew's version reflects a Palestinian setting: 'building on a rock,' 'a rainy season,' and 'high winds.' The foolish man builds his house on the edge of a wadi, which is dry during summer months but flowing with water during the rainy season.

"Luke's version, on the other hand, seems to reflect conditions more in keeping with a Greek setting. Luke speaks of 'digging and laying a foundation,' according to Greek building practices. He also makes an explicit reference to floods. Lastly, Luke drops reference to 'winds' and a 'rainy season.'

"Luke's differences do not change the meaning of Jesus' parable. The same point emerges: to listen to the words of Jesus and to admire his deeds is not enough. You must put them into practice in your life."

It is our belief that *Come Mime With Me* reflects the same approach to thinking and teaching of scripture that Mark Link envisions in the above story told two different ways. The deeper meaning of our dramas, and what's more important, the format, is very pointed, very spiritual, and accurate in conveying a scriptural message.

THE SIMPLER, THE BETTER

In our dealings with children, we've come to realize that many children go to school with a very low self-esteem. One way to instill confidence in any child (5 or 75) is through drama, especially pantomime. This mode of expression creatively leaves no room for failure. Success each and everytime! The need for props in a scriptural pantomime is negligible, as the participants, if encouraged properly, can become whatever they wish, even a purple-banded, yellow polkadotted top hat! Through facial expression and complete use of the body, we can convey a myriad of feelings. The focus should be on the person's ability to express and create silently as a story is narrated. Some simple props we use are as follows:

1. Bible

2. Make-up: Some dramas or liturgical mime call for the participant to make up their faces. We often use a white cross on the cheek, outlined in black. The point is to relay the message that I am different, I am becoming a leader, one who steps out, listens, and acts on the Word. A mask helps one to feel free. Behind a mask or make-up, we can be anything we want to be.

3. Mural paper (simple words or signs to represent theme).

4. Poster board, a hand carried prop depicting a particular theme, (this could be taped to the class yardsticks).

5. Hats, books, leaves, one toy or other simple item to explain the theme.

The adapted scripture examples we've given, beginning with the first drama, are those we've used with youngsters ranging in age from 5 to 75. In order to adapt scripture, we have used simple techniques developed over a period of two years.

Many methods of teaching scripture become complicated. Our aim in each drama, is to convey one simple message, one that is easily learned and applied to daily experiences. Remember, THE SIMPLER THE BETTER.

READY NOW!

ONE **TWO** **THREE**

LET'S PUT A DRAMA TOGETHER

Let's get to the business of putting a drama together. Simplicity is the key. The following is a step by step format that covers a production before, during and after.

PRELUDE

Become in tune with your environment i.e., school principal, staff, volunteers, students, etc. Through active communication, you will discover the issues that can be dealt with by scriptural drama. By doing this, the theme you choose will be apropos to what's happening.

PREPARATION

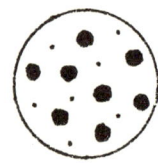

1. **Develop key words** that can be incorporated into the drama. These are based on the discovered needs of your environment.

2. **Keep resource books at your disposal.**

   A. Bible — it will provide a selection of scripture to meet specific needs.

   B. Thesaurus — to expand upon key words.

   C. Biblical Concordance — an excellent source of word or phrase scripture locations.

   D. Biblical Commentary — to expound upon a given scripture meaning.

3. **Read several or all of the biblical quotes you've located** and then choose one. This will enable you to home in on your theme. It is essential that the key words in scripture match those that you have previously developed. You will feel at peace with your selection if it is the one you are led to use by the Holy Spirit.

4. **Pray, think, ponder, compare,** or whatever you choose to call it. In the end, this step will lead you to a clearer understanding of how to mold your abstract feeling with the scriptures. Adaptation!

5. **Read the scripture again.** (Not to worry, God will do the rest.) Keep your pen and paper handy but step away and let all the above digest. As things come into your mind, jot them down.

WRITING

6. **Develop a story idea** that pertains to the specific need. Your paraphrased drama will evolve from the bank of personal experience.

7. **Good! Now you are writing.** Concentrate on substituting local persons, places and things for biblical. This is what adapted paraphrased scripture is.

8. **Keep it simple.** While remaining true to the scripture, are you using key words that will lead to a one-liner. Jesus' messages came through in brief parables. Your drama should follow suit.

9. **Finish your drama with:**

   A. "The moral of the story is ..." This uses the key words, the one-liner of your drama.

   B. "This has been a paraphrased scriptural drama according to God, (your name) and kids (whoever your cast is)." This emphasizes that it is not a word-for-word dramatization but a paraphrased rendition of God's Word. This also recognizes the glory goes to God and that you and the cast are simply his tools.

   C. Follow-Up Questions — Compile questions for the audience that will help to reinforce the one-liner message.

   D. Summary Statement — This should be very brief to cement the whole message of your paraphrased drama.

10. **Drama overview** (attending to the details):

    A. Drama statistics — title, scripture, theme, reason, key words, drama time, and by whom.

B. Cast list — character portrayed.

C. Physical props — Bible, etc.

D. Mimed props.

E. Special reminders — your own notes.

PRE-DRAMA

11. **To put the drama into action you must:**

   A. Select a place to practice and perform.

   B. Twenty minutes before drama go to the class with your props in hand ... or forty minutes prior, have kids make simple props. We often used items such as a mural, a set of keys, flash light etc. We also found that children enjoyed imitating real props through mimed action.

   C. Choose several children to portray persons, places and things in your drama.

   D. Choose your narrator, whether it is you, a student or other.

12. **Develop mime for narrated drama.** Include suggestions from the children, incorporating their creativity. Run through actions briefly. When practicing, the narrator should speak at a moderate tempo (matching pace of actors) and with clarity. The actors should offer the same courtesy to the narrator.

13. **If you are using props or simple make-up,** this is the time to put it all together.

14. **Pray with your cast** prior to actual performance, giving all glory to God.

SHOW TIME

15. **Now you are ready to create your own stage.** (Narrator enters)

    A. Narrator requests audience to *"pull down the shades"* (close eyes). This creates the illusion of a closed curtain.

    B. The cast enters and turns their backs to the audience, this adds to the appearance of a drawn curtain.

    C. When props are set up and the narration ready to begin, the narrator tells the audience to *"open shades"* (open eyes). This creates the illusion of the stage curtain rising.

16. **The drama unfolds**

    A. Narrator reads your chosen scripture. (Remember this is the scripture you have selected to meet the specific needs of your environment.)

    B. Narrator continues into the drama.

    C. As each cast member is mentioned in the storyline, he or she turns toward the audience and mimes his or her part.

17. **Close with the following:**

    A. The moral of the story (the one-liner) should be introduced through the use of clown antics: dancing forward, cupping a hand to the ear, spreading fingers, smiling, and in a sing-song voice saying, "The moral of the story is ..."

    B. Say: "This has been a paraphrased scriptural reading according to God, (your own name and grade or people in the cast)."

    C. An excellent reinforcement is to summarize with a song, one that pertains to the message just experienced. Use a taped song if you wish.

FOLLOW-UP

18. **There are two types of follow-up:**

    A. **Immediate:**

    1. Cover follow-up questions and summary statement immediately after the drama or sometime later in the day.

    2. Artwork can be assigned as an optional reinforcement to the message. Set a deadline for completed artwork. This is a good opportunity to give the shy child with low self-esteem a positive experience. Display art in a place of honor.

    3. Hand out the "Teachers Critique." (See sample on page 67.) This gives you feedback questions: Did the drama relate to scripture? Did the audience come away with key words and a one-liner? Was it simple enough to be easily applied and was it enjoyed?

    B. **One Week Later:**

    1. Go back, collect art work and critiques.

    2. Give a brief recap of drama by reviewing the moral, the follow-up questions and the summary.

19. **Congratulations!** You now have a drama that involves children and relates scripture to everyday life.

P.S.: Our simple prop selections, writing, drama techniques, and mimed actions can be used in a variety of liturgies. Any reading at a children's Christmas service, for example. Feel free to be creative and use the techniques that will best fit your group.

Now you are ready to begin anew for the next drama.

TITLE:	**SPREAD THE WORD**
SCRIPTURE:	1 Thessalonians 1:2-3,7-8
	NAB or The Way
THEME/REASON:	Feast of Peter and Paul
KEY PHRASE:	Action through example
DRAMA TIME:	15 minutes
BY:	God, Gail, Carol and kids

As this drama unfolds, the cast will, by character, turn towards the audience and perform action to fit the italicized instructions. Use your own imagination to add or delete actions.

CAST:

Peter Pauline
Peter's Friends (as many as you are comfortable working with)
Tommy
Ida
Ida's School Mates (as many as you are comfortable working with)
Leah from Los Angeles
Students to hold scenery

PHYSICAL PROPS:

1. Bible

2. Make-up paint (use to put a cross on cheek of each participant)

3. Large colorful banner depicting the theme

MIMED PROPS:

1. As discussed earlier, we are trying to simplify the use of physical props through the use of pantomime. Therefore, when the student is writing the thank yous, he can easily pantomime the use of a desk, pen, paper and window to gaze from.

2. Any created activity which will add to storyline.

• When writing the drama, frequently refer back to scripture, making sure you are saying the same thing in today's words. You need to be scripturally accurate.

• Use the key words during a question-answer session after the drama. These key words will come in handy for reinforcement, which will begin immediately after the drama and continue with follow-up a week later.

To Begin:

NARRATOR: *enters* and tells audience to "Pull Shades."
CAST: *enters* and turns back to the audience.
NARRATOR: says *"Open Shades,"* then *proceeds* with Scripture reading, followed by the narration.

Narration:

Peter Pauline was a fourth grader at St. Ann's School in Ridgecrest. Peter and *his friends* were good students and honest children who always *played* fun games. One day a student, *Tommy,* came to visit from the Trona School District. Because of the *good time* he had, Tommy decided to write a *thank you letter* to Peter. As he *sat down* and began to *daydream,* his words of thanks *began to flow.*

[other players lend an ear by leaning forward and cupping ear while listening]

"Dear Peter and friends. It was great to be a student at your school. I learned many things about people from Saint Ann's. Because of you and your friends, I learned much about being a good and honest kid, both on the school grounds and off. Tomorrow I'm telling my friends about you and the things that seem to make you all so different. Things like: not laughing at me when I didn't know what to do, and helping the volunteer parent load her car full of song books and telling me some of the good things you look for in a real friend. I better go now. Love ya, Tommy."

One day a student, *Ida,* came to Tommy's school and Tommy was to be her special helper. *They* had lots of *fun together* and *exchanged stories* of each other' schools. This student was from Inyokern and *upon returning there, wrote a thank you* to Tommy much the same as Peter Pauline had received. *Ida* from Inyokern *began her letter* this way.

[other players lend an ear]

"Hey Tommy, I want to thank you for many things. "Because you showed me how to be of help to strangers, lots of people here will be better off. I hope we can visit again soon. We became such good friends and I'm telling all the kids how fun and friendly you are. Your friend, Ida."

Some weeks later, *Ida* from Inyokern and *her schoolmates* were visited by yet another student, *Leah* from Los Angeles. *Ida invited her friends* over and *together they taught Leah* from Los Angeles a new form of *ball game* called, "pickle." *The thank you that followed Leah's visit* went like so ...

[other players lend an ear]

"Dear Ida and gang, thank you for buying me ice cream after lunch. I'm lucky I was there on such a fun day. You and your friends are special. Because you showed me kindness when I made dumb pickle plays, I promise to show kindness to others. I have already had many laughs with my friends as I tell them of the game and some of the mistakes I made. Love and Kisses, Leah from L.A.

[with a little more thought]

P.S. I'm thankful for the opportunity to visit and be a part of your school. The laughter we shared is sort of like spreading jelly!! You get a little on yourself and before you know it, it's everywhere. It not only sticks to you (jelly and niceness) but everything and everybody you touch."

[as the drama nears the end, our narrator reads the moral of the story as the cast listens attentively]

The Moral of the Story is:

1. By thinking of, being thankful for and remembering others' good actions, we can be "honest hope — JESUS" to students everywhere.

2. Something nice you do may spread everywhere like jelly.

3. News of your kindness will spread throughout the California school system, by your very own "good example."

This has been a para-phrased scriptural drama according to God, Gail, Carol and kids.

FOLLOW-UP QUESTIONS

1. Who was Peter and Paul? (Christ's specially chosen friends who taught about God's love through action and example.)

2. How could you spread God's word through example? (By not laughing at others when they make a mistake ... etc.)

SUMMARY STATEMENT

If Peter and Paul had not done their jobs of "spreading the Word" we wouldn't know of God's love and *how to* spread the example of his love to others.

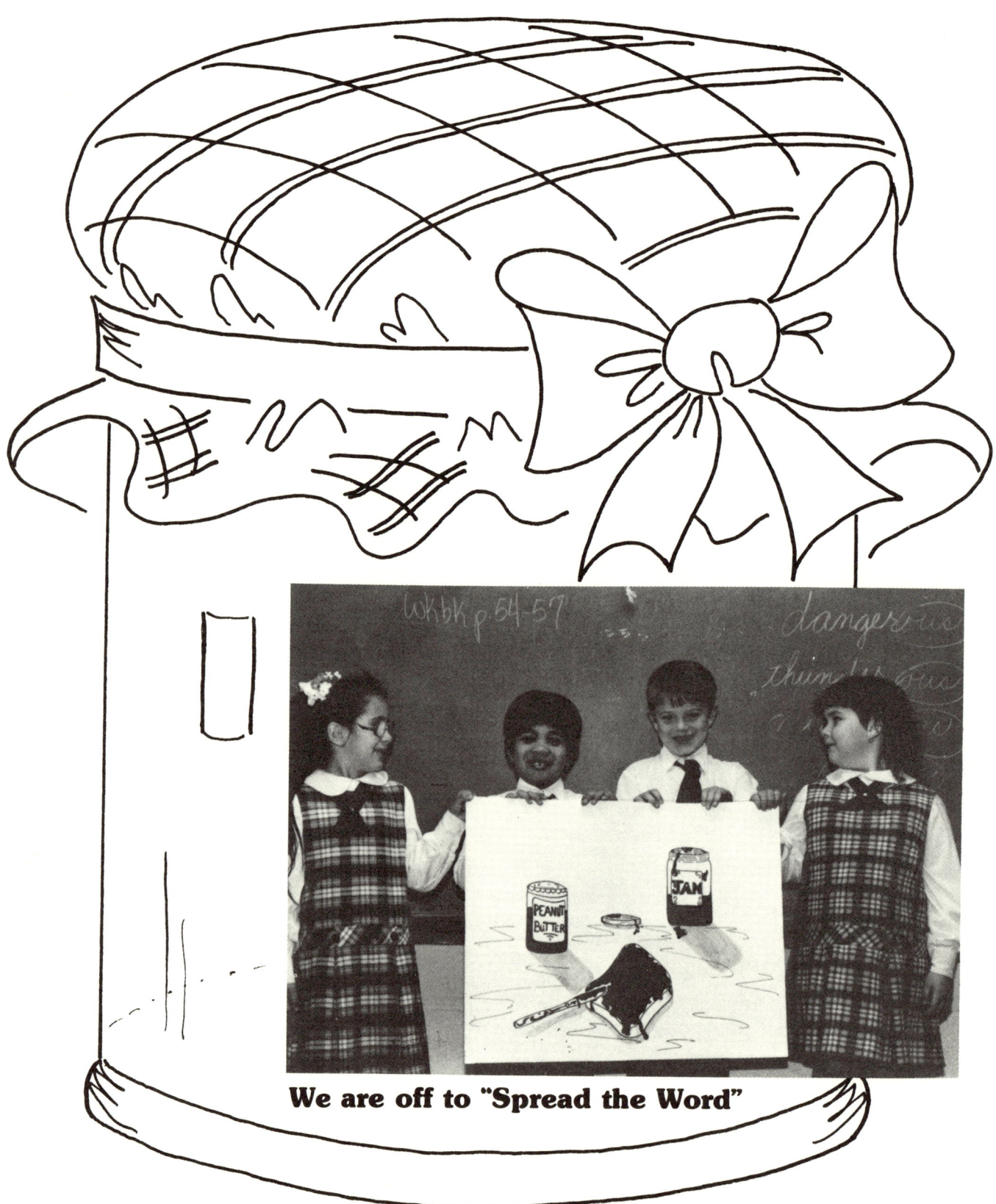

We are off to "Spread the Word"

ME USEFUL?!

or

"A Cactus Who Found His Place"

TITLE:		**ME USEFUL?**
SCRIPTURE:		Galatians 2:6-9
		The Living Bible
THEME:		Accepting that we have differences
REASON:		Beginning a new school year
KEY WORDS:		Welcome, purpose, and different
DRAMA TIME:		15-20 minutes
BY:		God, Gail, Carol and Kids

As this drama unfolds, the cast will, by character, turn towards the audience and perform action to fit the italicized instructions. Use your own imagination to add or delete actions.

CAST:

Gardener
Cactus
Roses (as many as you are comfortable working with)
Desert Traveler
Fence Holders (if you decide to use them)
Students to hold scenery

PHYSICAL PROPS:

1. Bible

2. Make-up paint (use this to put a cross on cheek of each participant)

3. Large colorful banners or posters depicting the theme.

4. Plastic garden fence to set stage, easily held in place with extra children. Should you be able to perform outside on a nice lawn, then simply stick the fence into the ground.

5. Garden tools if you wish.

MIMED PROPS:

1. If physical props are not used, you can play-act the use of garden tools.

2. Add any extra activity that will enhance the authenticity of the storyline.

• Remember to refer back to scripture frequently. Being scripturally accurate is of the utmost importance.

(or A CACTUS WHO FOUND HIS PLACE)

- Use the key words as a question-answer session after the drama. These key words will come in handy for reinforcement which will begin immediately after the drama and continue with the follow-up a week later.

- Whenever a narrator's thought is to be interjected into the drama, it will be put in a set of double parentheses (( ))s.

TO BEGIN:

NARRATOR: *enters* and tells audience to "Pull Shades."
CAST: *enters* and *turns back* to the audience.
NARRATOR: says *"Open Shades,"* then *proceeds* with scripture reading, followed by the narration.

NARRATION:

Once upon a time there was a *gardener* who spent his day, from sunup to sundown, *working* in his garden. He *did many things* to make his garden the best in the desert. Even though the *soil was dry and very hard*, the gardener knew it could produce beautiful roses. He not only loved to look at the flowers, but enjoyed their lovely smell.

    [gardener goes about business of working in
    garden]

The time had come for the *gardener to cultivate the soil* and make it ready for the planting. *He dug up the soil, watered it* with good rain water, and then *went about buying and planting the roses. The roses were short and thin* at first, but with *gentle care*, they *began to fill out*.

    [roses notice cactus grow]
    [gardener also takes curious notice]

Somehow the garden also *produced a cactus*, and a *very healthy one* at that. The *gardener saw* the *critter sprouting among his roses* and, after *thinking about it*, decided to let it grow. ((I guess he realized that even though the cactus was quite different from the roses, it had a beauty all its own and would contribute to the overall character of the garden.)) When all of the gardener's work was done, *he went to rest under the shade of a big tree*.

    [all show moving signs of growing life]

The *roses were priding themselves* on their outward *beauty* and terrific *smell*, momentarily forgetting about the stranger in their midst. As they were doing this, the *cactus looked about*, and wondered, "How in the name of St. Anne did

I ever get here? After all, *I don't have pretty flower petals* and *I don't smell nice,* like the others. I certainly *don't have a slender graceful body* like the roses around me."

   [roses look in amazement]
   [roses gradually come to senses]

With that, *he pulled himself up, roots and all* to find *another place in which to grow.* As he left, *the roses noticed a great sadness* coming over them and *they began to wilt.* ((For you see, the root system of each plant helped the other to grow. I guess maybe they helped make the soil better for each other.)) When the *roses came to their senses,* they realized they hadn't made the cactus feel fully welcome and needed. Upon realizing this, *they coaxed the cactus* into *coming* and *sharing the garden* once more.

   [the now Happy Garden continues growing; at the
   same time they notice a rather tired looking
   traveler appearing on the scene]

One very sunny, hot desert day, a *thirsty and weary traveler happened upon* the beautiful *garden. He desperately needed something to satisfy his thirst. The traveler had come a long way and had quite a distance yet to go.* He was very good with plants and knew, as Dr. Dolittle did, how to talk to the plants. *Relaxing himself* and *thinking thoughts* of the garden he asked this question. *"I'm so thirsty, can any of you help me out?"*

   [all lend an ear to the traveler, then to the cactus]

The *cactus called out,* "Hey, the fact that I'm different is going to really be wonderful for you. *I don't have the pretty rose petals,* but *I do have a lot of water in my branches* and would be happy to *let you take a piece of me and drink.*

   [as the traveler drinks, the roses show their pride in
   the cactus by giving him lots of sticky hugs]
   [All watch as traveler finishes drink]

Tasting of the energy giving water, our traveler felt strong enough to complete his journey. So off into the HOT sunset he walked, over the hills past Cerro Coso College, with a fond memory of the roses and the cactus.

> [roses and cactus watch the traveler leave and see the gardener awaken and come back to check the garden.]

As the *gardener returned, he noticed* something different and beautiful about *his garden.* That funny looking and oddly placed *cactus had burst into bloom. The gardener's last thought* was, "Boy, am I glad I decided to let him grow in my garden."

> [all lend an ear]

The moral of the story is:

1. Even though we are all different, we have a contribution to make wherever we are planted.

2. Each of us have different qualities and God meant for us to use them for the good of each other.

This has been a paraphrased scriptural drama according to God, Gail, Carol, and Kids.

FOLLOW-UP QUESTIONS

1. Do you welcome those who appear to be different? (ask for examples)

2. Do you realize that God made each of us different and with a purpose? (ask for examples)

SUMMARY STATEMENT

Just as we all are the same in God's eyes, and needed for our differences, so too were the roses and cactus appreciated and needed for their differences.

"We found our place"

C.T., J.C., and ME

TITLE:	**C.T., J.C., AND ME**
SCRIPTURE:	Matthew 5:14-16 John 8:12 Living Bible or NAB
THEME/REASON:	Now that we know we are accepted, what do we do with our talents?
KEY PHRASE:	decision to help, let others see God's glory and goodness through you
DRAMA TIME:	15 minutes
BY:	God, Gail, Carol and kids

As this drama unfolds, the cast will, by character, turn towards the audience and perform action to fit the italicized instructions. Use your own imagination to add or delete actions.

CAST:

Mel
Emily
C.T.
J.C.
Students to hold scenery and flashlight

PHYSICAL PROPS:

1. Bible

2. Make-up paint (use to put a cross on cheek of each participant)

3. Poster boards attached to class yard sticks with simple but colorful scenes: spaceship, C.T., planet Shine-On

4. Large oversized C.T. nametag

5. Flashlight to shine on C.T.'s picture (poster) and to aid in his "glow."

MIMED PROPS:

1. Miming the spaceship, trail, stream, store, etc., can effectively be done by the students whom you choose to hold the poster board (i.e. the spaceship could easily land/enter/turn towards audience with much fanfare). This becomes a combination physical and mimed prop.

2. Add any created activity of yours which will add to the storyline.

• When writing the drama, frequently refer back to scripture, making sure you are saying the same thing in today's words. You need to be scripturally accurate.

- Remember to always use your key words for the question-answer session after the drama. This will be part of the Follow-Up.

- Whenever a narrator's thought is to be interjected into the drama, it will be put in a set of double (())s.

To Begin:

NARRATOR: *Enters* and tells audience to "Pull Shades."
CAST: *enters* and *turns back* to audience.
NARRATOR: says *"Open Shades"*, then *proceeds* with scripture reading, followed by narration.

Narration:

Once, sometime in the future, a supersonic spaceship *carried* two exploring kids to the much publicized planet of Shine-On. Mel and Emily wanted to spend some of their vacation exploring this planet they'd heard so much about and to discover the "secret of the glow."

> [children glance out window of ship as they fly over]

When the space craft *docked*, the boy and girl *stepped out* with caution. As they began to *explore* the land, they were surprised to see that the planet's air, ground, and water were much the same as on their own. There must be more to Shine-On than meets the eye, so off the children *hiked* to the nearest trail.

> [children explore towards trail]

It was great fun *exploring*. As the two *walked* further, they happened upon a *fast moving stream*. It looked so inviting that they *took off their shoes, rolled up their space pants and jumped right in*. During their *play*, Emily *slipped and fell*, injuring her ankle. *Mel told* her to sit on the rock by the stream and *soak her ankle* in cool water; while *he went to look for help*.

> [girl soaks ankle, boy goes for help]
> [girl becomes motionless as the next scene is enacted]

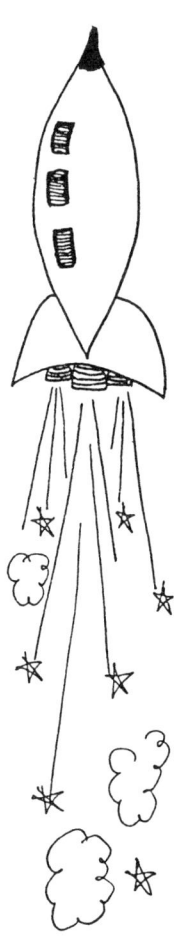

Remembering he'd seen an A.M.-P.M. Mini-Mart, as they flew over the area, the boy decided to *go back down the trail, past the spaceship to the store.* There he could seek help and buy some energy bars and travelaid juice.

[boy travels to market and shops]

Rushing to the market, Mel soon found himself *choosing some* very *delicious snacks.* The young *traveler noticed,* as he stepped up to the counter, that the cashier was the oddest, most unusual, barely glowing space creature he'd ever seen. ((Believe you me, he's seen a lot.)) *Mel gave the cashier* his space tokens, and *started out the door.*

[boy re-enters the market]

He was so curious about the cashier's appearance, that he nearly forgot to ask for help. *Back into the store he went,* quickly telling the cashier his story, hoping the clerk would help out.

[boy talking C.T. into helping]

The cashier, on whose nametag was written C.T., was shy about helping people he didn't know. Finally C.T. consented to *close the store* and go to the aid of the girl. ((Funny thing, C.T.'s glow began to brighten as the two *made their way down the road, past the spaceship, up the trail to the stream* where the girl sat soaking her ankle. This was the first time that C.T. had worked up the courage to share his powerful light from within, which all Shine-Oneons are famous for. Fear had kept his talents neatly hidden, but now he was choosing to share his healing light, which the children would see.))

[C.T. and boy wind their way to stream]

When they reached Emily, C.T. again became nervous and decided to *use his remote control transmitter* ((which was always in his back pocket)) to PHONE HOME! ((He knew his dad, J.C., would fill him with lots of encouraging words. Everytime they talked, C.T. felt his shining light from within generate an overpowering energy from his dad!)) When *J.C. answered* and heard the problem, he lovingly but firmly said, "C.T. we've talked of the time when you would share your powerful glow from within and now the time is at hand. You must look inside of yourself to discover your own glow, one that all Shine-Oneons are given and then use it with confidence for others."

[C.T. in conversation with J.C., away from rest of cast]
[boy and girl sit by stream]

((C.T. will discover that his healing "secret of the glow" is found when he opens up to the power of goodness, love and kindness that is given to all. Besides helping others he will discover that to use this power and to show it will bring to him, not only a shine but a bright outer glow that all can see. This is something that all Shine-Oneons strive for.))

[child now turns flashlight on C.T.'s poster]

When their conversation was over, *C.T. joined the children* by the stream, thought very hard about the "secret of the glow," *reached for the girl's ankle,* touched it and *helped her* to her feet!

[C.T., boy and girl walk toward the space craft]

As the *three worked their way to the spacecraft,* C.T. shared with them his discovery and hoped they too would one day find, in themselves, the "secret of the glow." ((C.T., by making a decision to touch others with his healing light learned a grand lesson that day.)) *Before boarding, they embraced each other.* The kids were glad they'd chosen Shine-On to visit and, as they blasted off, *they waved good-bye* to their brightly shining new friend. The children had come to see the power and love of J.C. through the goodness of C.T. Now they knew what the "secret of the glow" was, where it came from and what a powerful thing it could become.

[all lend an ear]

The moral of this story is:

1. We must discover our own talents. Something given to us all by a good and loving God.

2. When we realize what we have to offer others, we must share in God's Glory by using them and letting others see God's Power through us.

This has been a paraphrased scriptural drama according to God, Gail, Carol and kids.

FOLLOW-UP QUESTIONS

1. What is the secret of the glow? (God's loving power shining through us.)

2. How could you share the secret of YOUR glow? (ask for examples)

3. Who does J.C. remind you of?

SUMMARY STATEMENT

Because J.C. was such a good father, C.T. was able to share his loving glow for all to see and to benefit from. The children realized that the healing came from J.C. and they were thankful for it.

We too should let God's power help us discover our talents so that all may see the glory of God through us.

We Will Let Our Talents "Shine On"

THE ONE GREAT HOLY SPIRIT

TITLE:	**THE ONE GREAT**
SCRIPTURE:	John 14: 18-20 NIV or New Jerusalem
THEME/REASON:	Halloween and relating the spirits of saints to today and to God's Holy Spirit
KEY PHRASE:	Saints of heaven and earth Feeling the spirit of Jesus
DRAMA TIME:	15 minutes
BY:	God, Gail, Carol and kids

As this drama unfolds, the cast will, by character, turn towards the audience and perform action to fit the italicized instructions. Use your own imagination to add or delete actions.

CAST:

Juggling Clown
Dancing Clown
Magician Clown
Other town clowns (as many as you are comfortable with — they will take part in the actions where appropriate)
Students holding banner

PHYSICAL PROPS:

1. Bible

2. Make-up (use to put a cross on cheek of each participant)

3. Large colorful banner depicting theme

MIMED PROPS:

1. As discussed earlier, we are trying to simplify the use of physical props through the use of pantomime. In the case of the great and terrible storm, the children holding the banner could be thrashed about, falling to the ground, becoming the fallen tent. This is a combined physical/mimed prop.

2. Add any activity which will add to the storyline.

   • When writing the drama, frequently refer back to scripture, making sure you are saying the same thing in today's words. You need to be scripturally accurate.

   • Use the key words as a question-answer session after the drama. These

HOLY SPIRIT

key words will come in handy for reinforcement, which will begin immediately after the drama and continue with follow-up a week later.

• Whenever a narrator's thought is to be interjected into the drama, it will be put in a set of double (( ))s.

To Begin:

NARRATOR: *enters* and *tells* audience to *"Pull Shades."*
CAST: *enters* and *turns back* to audience.
NARRATOR: *says "Open Shades,"* then *proceeds* with Scripture reading, followed by narration.

NARRATOR: ((This is a time of year when all children bubble with the excitement of Halloween. It is a special time of year when spirits come to our minds and to our very doors expecting treats. The whole idea of the spirits at Halloween is taken from hundreds of years ago, when children used to dress as saints to drive away any unclean spirits. Today we dress as all sorts of funny and scary things. Halloween is really the eve before a great church holiday, sorta like Christmas Eve. The day following Halloween is quite special in the life of the church, a day when we honor the Saints of God, the special people like St. Francis or St. Ann. These people are now with God, at the same time they are still with us. We are all called to be saints or blessed or special people of God. The spirit of these saints lives with us today, in our hearts, in our own spirit and in our minds. It is up to us to invite the presence of their goodness into our lives.

Narration:

Excitement was on the rise in this town of clowns. The time had come for all the circus clowns to do what they did best.

[specific characters perform their part]

We have a *juggling clown, a dancing clown, and a magician clown.* Besides being very good jugglers and dancers and magicians, these clowns were the favorite of the circus people. ((In the circus, the best act is always saved for the last, and being the favorite, these clowns were chosen to lead the "Grand Finale."))

[clowns lead a make-believe line of all performers in "Grand Finale"]

Many things set these clowns apart. For one thing, they *shared everything, even their make-up.*

[All clowns go into audience and put a white face-paint cross on various people, using the paint from their own faces.]

The clowns also realized *smiles* are good ways to tell people they are important and good performers. I even heard that the *dancing clown taught* another clown his *new step.* ((They were special clowns alright — special enough to affect the lives of all the others. The favorite ones just seemed to have a certain something!))

[all clowns gather together and lend an ear as magician acts out his part]

The clown that was most popular was the magician clown. There were so many things he did well, such as:

Having some special *mud that he used* to heal *eye sicknesses.* He used it on many people who would go out and share their happiness.

He had many hand made *toys and chose to share them* with the young children of the circus, in hopes they too would share.

There was even a special book he used when people were tempted to do unkind things. All he had to do was *read them the words of goodness* and it seemed to make them stronger. They became more willing to try again, in order to earn the honor of being in the "Grand Finale."

[all clowns help set up tent and get ready for act]
[all make motions of being blown by storm]

Before all the clowns were to appear in the center ring, to do what they did best, a *great and terrible storm overcame the large tent.* Most of the clowns escaped serious injury, all except the *magician clown. He was trapped under a great beam,* was badly injured and needed to be rushed to the hospital ((much like the Drummond Medical Center)). Naturally *everyone was upset* by the accident and *went to see him every day.*

[magician talks to them from his bed]

The *magician clown was not well* and would have to remain in the hospital! All the *clowns were sad and wondered* what they would do without him. The *magician* said, "Even though I may not be living next door to you, please know my spirit, my love, will always be with you. I will never be away from you. I will be here in your heart, your spirit of goodness, to hear your troubles, to share your sorrows and your joys and to teach you the Words of Goodness. Remember me and the things we shared and you will feel my Presence when you are in need."

[all clowns hold hands waiting for narration to finish]

The moral of this story is:

1. God will not leave us alone. He will give to us the One Great Holy Spirit through Jesus Christ.

2. As with the saints of heaven and earth, their spirit lives on in us. We must allow the Holy Spirit of God to work in and through us, just as the magician would continue to help the town's clowns.

This has been a paraphrased scriptural drama according to God, Gail, Carol and kids.

FOLLOW-UP QUESTIONS

1. What have we learned from the Saints and made a part of us? (St. Clare — stepped out in faith and did the will of God. Father Kolbe — self sacrifice)

2. Have you ever felt God's presence, even though you haven't seen or felt him with "skin on"? (HOLY SPIRIT)

3. Which clown reminds you of the Holy Spirit?

SUMMARY STATEMENT

When the magician said, "You will Feel my Presence when you are in need, so will you also feel the presence of the Holy Spirit, a gift from God.

We Feel His "Presence"

They Shared Something TOGETHER

41

TITLE:	**THEY SHARED**
SCRIPTURE:	Col. 3:15-17
	NIV or The Way
THEME/REASON:	Thanksgiving Mass
KEY WORDS/PHRASE:	teach each other, we are one body, giving and thanks
DRAMA TIME:	7-10 minutes
BY:	God, Gail, Carol and kids

As the drama unfolds, the cast will, by character, turn towards the audience and perform action to fit the italicized instructions. Use your own imagination to add or delete actions.

CAST:

Scene 1: boy and girl
Scene 2: boy, mother and dad
Scene 3: mom, dad, girl and boy
Scene 4: all of the above come together to form ONE BODY IN CHRIST
students to hold scenery

PHYSICAL PROPS:

1. Bible

2. make-up (use this to put a cross on cheek of each player)

3. banner depicting theme. Remember to keep it simple!

MIMED PROPS:

1. By play acting the raking of leaves, taking medication, preparing the meal, and coming together as a community, you can do away with any physical props.

2. Add any extra activity that will enhance the authenticity of the storyline.

• Remember to refer back to scripture frequently. Being scripturally accurate is of the utmost importance.

• Use the key words as a question-answer session after the drama. These key words will come in handy for reinforcement, which will begin immediately after the drama and continue with the follow-up a week later.

SOMETHING TOGETHER

- Whenever a narrator's thought is to be interjected into the drama, it will be put in double (())s.

- Like the other short dramas, this can be used at Sunday service, mass, or in place of dinner prayer at a Cub Scout meeting.

To Begin:

NARRATOR: *enters* and tells audience to *"Pull Shades."*
CAST: *enters* and turns back to the audience.
NARRATOR: says *"Open Shades,"* then *proceeds* with scripture reading, followed by the narration.

Narration:

In our first scene we have a *brother and a sister* who are very *thankful* for the fallen leaves. They not only get to share the job of *raking up the colored leaves*, but share in the fun of *diving into the pile.* They shared something, TOGETHER. ((their family unity))

 [as children's part ends, they lend an ear and
 become motionless as next act is performed]

Secondly, we have a *boy who is ill* and *thankful that his parents* take such good care of him. Some of their concerns for the boy are making sure that he *eats the right food, takes his medication* and *has someone to color with.* They shared something, TOGETHER. ((their family unity))

 [as children's part ends, they lend an ear and
 become motionless as next act is performed]

Next the scene is set for a great feast. *Thanksgiving is here* and dinner is nearly ready. *Mom has done the cooking* and *dad is carving the turkey.* The *sister teaches* the brother how to properly set the table and the *brother will now lead* in the Thanksgiving prayer/song before they eat. They shared something, TOGETHER. ((their family unity))

 [as this scene ends, all children come together,
 face audience, hold hands and wait with lending
 ears as narration ends]

Lastly we *see another kind of sharing*. At church *we become One Body in Christ*. We should listen to God's Word and feel happy about our experiences together. Teach one another and praise and thank God joyously TOGETHER, through Jesus, for all our many gifts. We share something, TOGETHER. ((our family unity))

[all lend an ear]

The moral of this story is:
1. We are called to be One in the Lord.

2. We must come together as a family unit in thanksgiving.

3. We are instructed to help each other in many ways — in word, deed, natural family, and church family.

This has been a para-phrased scriptural drama according to God, Gail, Carol and kids.

FOLLOW-UP QUESTIONS

1. How many of you go to mass and feel like a member of the church family?

2. Do you make the person next to you feel at home?

3. Whether in word or deed do we say thanks to God in the name of Jesus?

SUMMARY STATEMENT

Just as you and your natural family work and play and eat together, so too should you come together in a church community. The reason for our being together at church is to become one body in Christ.

TOGETHER

We Are "One Body In Christ"

INVITE THEM IN

TITLE:	**INVITE THEM IN**
SCRIPTURE:	Matthew 9:13-14
	The Way or Good News
THEME/REASON:	Come to Jesus with the excitement of children
KEY WORDS:	trust, excitement, wonder
DRAMA TIME:	10 minutes
BY:	God, Gail, Carol and kids

As the drama unfolds, the cast will, by character, turn towards the audience and perform action to fit the italicized instructions. Use your own imagination to add or delete actions.

CAST:

Mr. Dan Clark
young students (as many as you can work with)
teachers
students to hold scenery

PHYSICAL PROPS:

1. Bible

2. Make-up paint (use to put a cross on cheek of each participant)

3. Large banner colorfully decorated depicting the theme

4. Keys for Mr. Clark to unlock door

MIMED PROPS:

1. As discussed earlier, we are trying to simplify the use of physical props through the use of pantomime.

2. Use any action to create a person, place or thing that will add to the story line.

• When writing the drama, frequently refer back to scripture, making sure you are saying the same thing only in todays words. You need to be scripturally accurate.

• Use the key words as a question-answer session after the drama. These key words will come in handy for reinforcement which will begin immediately after the drama and continue with the follow-up a week later.

• Whenever a narrator's thought is to be interjected into the drama, it will be put in double (())s.

To Begin:

NARRATOR: *enters* and tells audience to *"Pull Shades."*
CAST: *enters* and *turns back* to audience.
NARRATOR: says *"Open Shades,"* then *proceeds* with Scripture reading, followed by narration.

Narration:

It was early one December morning when Mr. Clark, the principal, *arrived at school*. He had a full day of teaching and principalizing ahead of him. He was *full of energy* and began his day by *teaching* a reading comprehension class and *coaching* St. Ann's basketball team.

[principal goes to lounge]

As the morning came to a close, he *went to the teachers lounge* and began to *eat the lunch* his wife Pammie fixed. His *spirits were high* but his *energy level took a definite downswing*.

[he begins to show signs of tiredness]

After lunch, Dan *went back to the office* to meet deadlines, deal with parents and to make decisions about the new reading program. Mr. Clark began to feel very tired. He *was so tired* that he *fell asleep* for a few moments as he was reading the last memo from yesterday's board meeting.

[awakens to bell]

The three thirty bell rang. What a great time of day. Yes, quitting time finally had arrived. Dan was *locking up his office door* when *some excited kindergardners came running up to him*. Their bus had not arrived yet so they decided to stop by and *chat*.

[Clark and kids talk, teachers shoo kids away]

Well the *teachers who were still at school, tried to rush ((nicely)) the children away,* for they knew how tired Mr. Clark was. It was tempting for Dan to let this happen. After all, he really was beat. With a little bit of energy and in a spirit of love he said, "I don't mind. Come on in kids."

[talks with teachers and asks kids in]

As he *unlocked his door, Mr. Clark invited the children into his office.* They all sat down and within minutes the *kids were asking questions.*

"I know my teacher said this is a special time of the year,
but I forgot! What is it?" "How long does Advent last?"
"Who did she say was coming?"

((You know, as they talked, Dan could see in the kids a sense of belief and trust in what he said. That made Dan want to share his office with them more often.))

[finish talk and kids go to playground]

With their questions answered, the *children gave Mr. Clark a big hug and smile, waved good-bye and ran to the playground* to wait for their bus.

[Mr. Clark in thought]

Sitting back and thinking, he was thankful for the chance to be with the little children, for it was he that learned something that day. Their questions, wonder, excitement, and trust was a great way to end his day. He even *made a promise to himself* to put some of their childlike excitement and trust back into his adult life.

[all lend an ear]

The moral of this story is:

1. Christ wants us to know him with the eagerness of a child.

2. We as adults have much to relearn from the little children.

3. To the little children belongs the kingdom of heaven.

This has been a para-phrased scriptural drama according to God, Gail, Carol and kids.

FOLLOW-UP QUESTIONS

1. Can you give an example of a time when you have felt the excitement, wonder and trust of a little child?

2. Have you ever made the same discovery that Mr. Clark did?

SUMMARY STATEMENT

Because Dan did not turn the children away, he learned much from their childlike eagerness. Christ also welcomes ALL to his Kingdom, especially those who come as trusting little children.

St. Ann's School

"We Trust Him"

MORE TIMES THAN YOU CAN COUNT

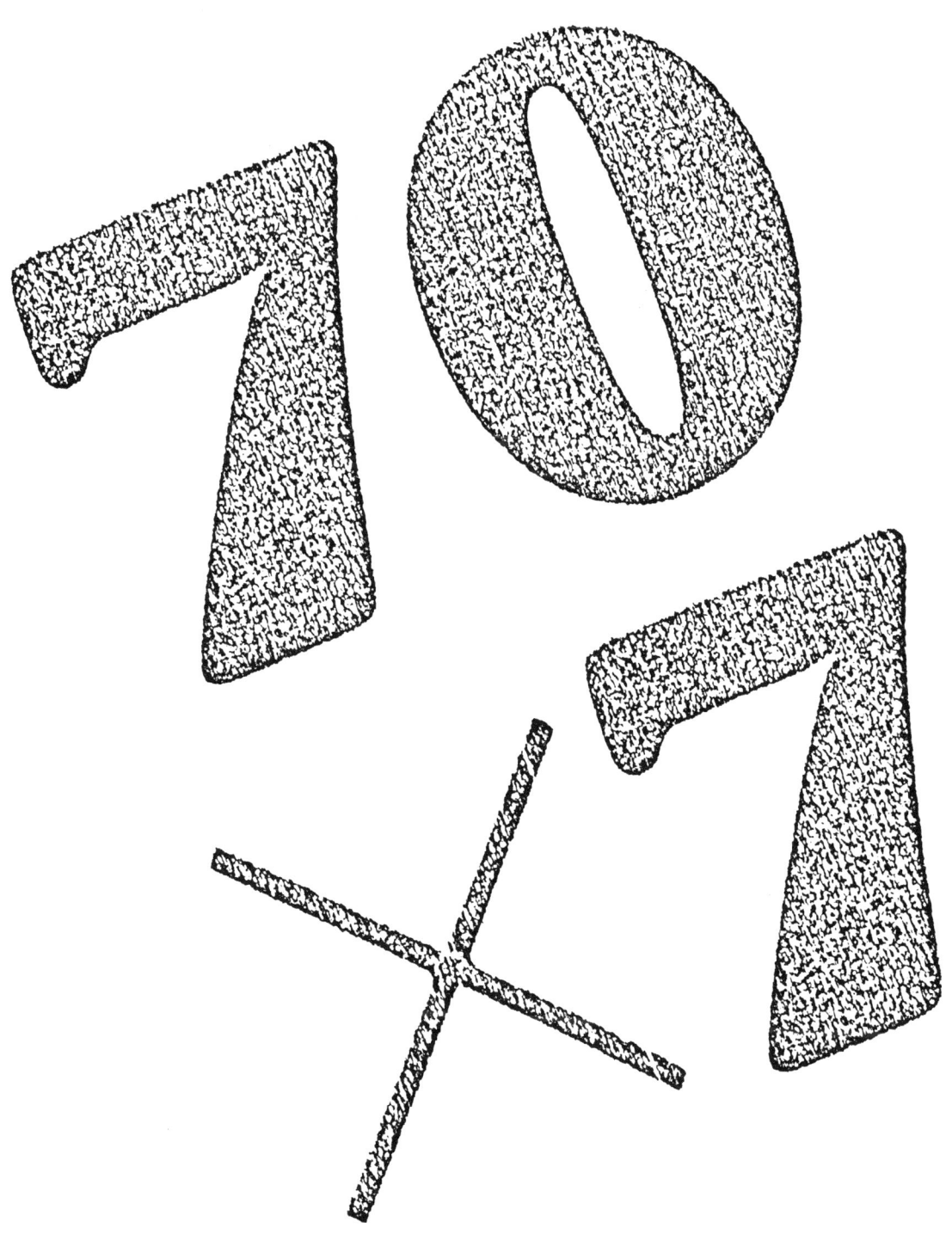

TITLE:	**MORE TIMES THAN**
SCRIPTURE:	Matthew 18:21,22, 33
	Jerusalem
THEME/REASON:	Forgiveness
KEY PHRASE:	to forgive more than once
DRAMA TIME:	10 minutes
BY:	God, Gail, Carol and kids

As this drama unfolds, the cast will, by character, turn towards the audience and perform action to fit the italicized instructions. Use your own imagination to add or delete actions.

CAST:

teasing child
schoolmates (specific actions listed in drama)
shy child
teacher (only one)
new student
students to hold banner

PHYSICAL PROPS:

1. Bible

2. Make-up paint (use to put a cross on cheek of each participant)

3. Large banner or poster colorfully decorated for theme.

MIMED PROPS:

1. By simplifying the use of physical props through the use of pantomime, we play-act the use of a phone, pencil, etc.

2. Add any extra activity that will enhance the authenticity of the storyline.

• Remember to refer back to scripture frequently. Being scripturally accurate is of the utmost importance.

• Use the key words as a question-answer session after the drama. These key words will come in handy for reinforcement, which will begin immediately after the drama and continue with the follow-up a week later.

• Whenever a narrator's thought is to be interjected into the drama, it will be put into a set of double (())s.

YOU CAN COUNT

To Begin:

NARRATOR: *Enters* and tells audience to *"Pull Shades."*
CAST: *enters* and *turns back* to the audience.
NARRATOR: says *"Open Shades,"* then *proceeds* with the scripture reading, followed by the narration.

Narration:

Once there was a child who always *teased*. This child went to school in a valley just like Indian Wells. He had friends for a long time until, one day, the child *teased once too often!* Some of the aggravating things he did to his schoolmates were;

> *hide their pencils*
> *put dust in their hair*
> *call them on the phone and then hang up*
> *tell white lies to teachers and friends*
> *talk about people*

> [children being teased meet and mime actions]
> [teaser becomes still]

This continued until the schoolmates finally *meet* on the playground, deciding *to expel* the teaser from their group and *to ignore* the child completely. They really weren't going to take this any longer.

> [shy boy becomes heard]

There was a *shy boy* who *listened* to all of the talk and nearly always agreed with the decisions of the crowd, that is until *he remembered* the words his dad so often says, "Kill 'em with kindness." ((His dad figured that if you were nice to someone more times than they could count, they were bound to change.)) The *shy boy told* the others of his thoughts and their final decision was to give the teaser another chance.

> [each individually act out part]

57

So when the teaser started *hiding pencils again,* his *classmates told* him to keep them.

[each individual acts out part]

So when *the teaser threw dirt* in the hair of a classmate, *he shook it out* and *told* the teaser, "I don't like you doing that, but I'm going to try to like you anyway."

[each individual acts out part]

So when the *teaser was a nag on the phone,* the *children would answer back with a friendly,* "Have a nice day."

[each individual acts out part]

So when the *teaser told lies* to the teacher and kids, they would *tell* this child, "I know you lied, but I can handle that. We all do it sometimes."

[each individual acts out part]

So when the *teaser talked about children behind their backs,* they would *respond with caring notes decorated with hearts.*

[all lend an ear]

((Well you can imagine what all this forgiveness did to the teaser. It positively blew his mind! He, without knowing it, grew to know what real happy hearted forgiveness meant. Although there wasn't one particular day that I can say the teaser grew the most, the child did in fact change. Guess the shy boy's father was right.))

[all lend an ear as new student and teaser mime actions]

Can you imagine this? One day a *new student arrived* at school. From the very beginning, he started throwing dirt at anyone who got within firing range. The *changed teaser said,* "I don't like you doing that, but I am going to try to like you anyway," and off he went to play.

[all lend an ear as moral is read]

The moral of this story is:

1. To forgive others, more times than you can count, will change a person for the better.

2. It is up to us to forgive others as we have been forgiven.

This has been a parapharased scriptural drama according to God, Gail, Carol and kids.

FOLLOW-UP QUESTIONS

1. Have you been forgiven for something you have done to someone more than once? (ask for specific examples)

2. Have you ever forgiven someone for the same thing more than once? (ask for specific examples)

SUMMARY STATEMENT

The children responded to the teaser with forgiveness more than once. In turn the teaser shared that lesson of forgiveness with another. Christ teaches us to forgive the same way we are forgiven. Not once but SEVENTY TIMES SEVEN!

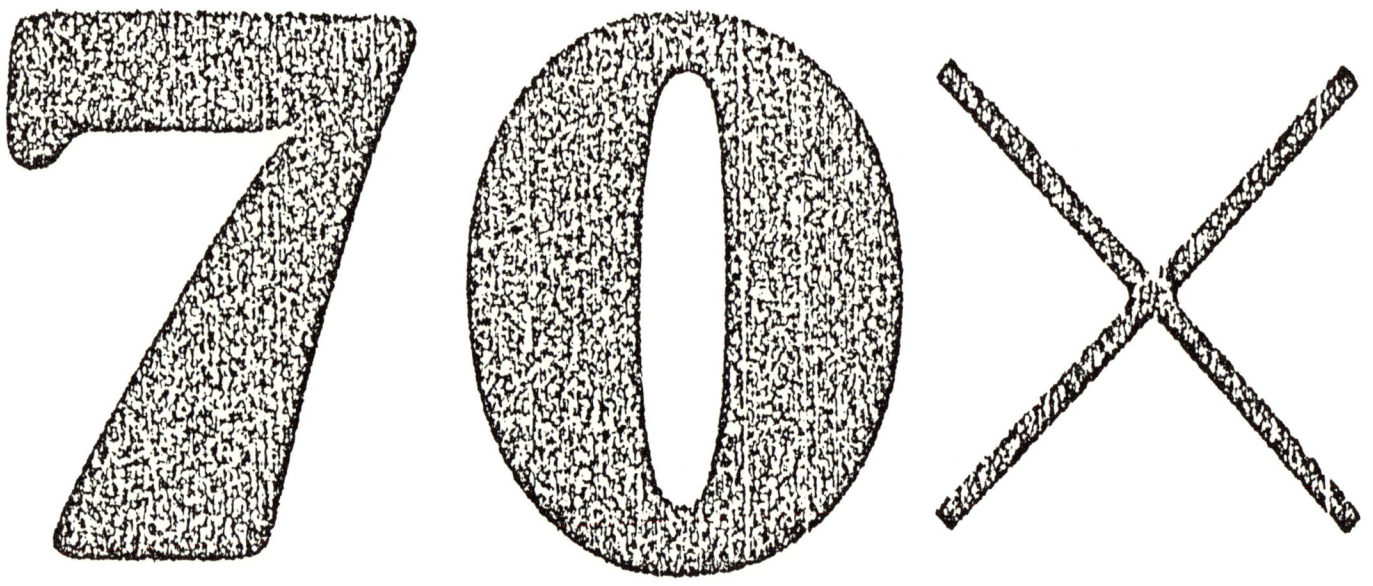

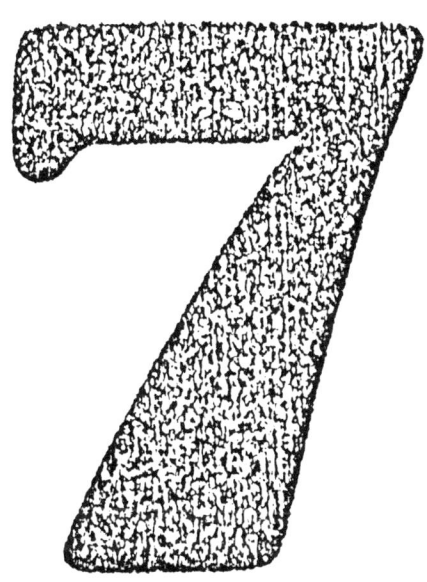

"We Forgive"
"We Are Forgiven"

STRAIGHT But NARROW

TITLE: **STRAIGHT BUT NARROW**

SCRIPTURE:	John 1:23 Luke 13:24 Jerusalem/Good News
THEME:	Preparation
REASON:	Clearing life's obstacles to God
KEY WORDS:	prepare, make plans, build, getting home
DRAMA:	15 minutes
BY:	God, Gail, Carol and kids

As this drama unfolds, the cast will, by character, turn towards the audience and perform action to fit the italicized instructions. Use your own imagination to add or delete actions.

CAST:

father
family (as many as you can handle)
carpenter friend
airplane pilot
bulldozer
students to hold scenery

PHYSICAL PROPS

1. Bible

2. make-up (use this to put a cross on cheek of each participant)

3. large banner or posters colorfully decorated, depicting the theme.

4. phone to make phone calls

MIMED PROPS:

1. Simplifying the use of physical props through pantomime, we play act the use of a phone and other items.

2. Add any extra activity that will enhance the authenticity of the storyline.

• Remember to refer back to scripture frequently. Being scripturally accurate is of the utmost importance.

• Use the key words as a question-answer session after the drama. They will come in handy for reinforcement which will begin immediately after the drama and continue with the follow-up a week later.

• Whenever a narrator's thought is to be interjected into the drama, it will be put in a set of double (())s.

To Begin:

NARRATOR: *Enters* and tells audience to *"Pull Shades."*
CAST: *enters* and *turns back* to the audience.
NARRATOR: says *"Open Shades,"* then *proceeds* with the scripture reading, followed by the narration.

Narration:

Living in the city is fun and exciting. There are many things to do and see. As a matter of fact, one family I know did many things to entertain themselves.

Going to the movie every Friday night.
Playing miniature golf on Saturday.
Going to the zoo during the summer.

[family tires of city life and decides otherwise]

Over the years the *family tired* of the noise and fast pace of city life. *They decided* to build their own special home in an area surrounded by nature ((for this was one thing the city lacked)). It would take some doing, so the *father began to think and to make plans.*

[father remembers school friend]

He remembered an old school friend who had chosen a life much different than the city life he'd been living. *His friend had become a carpenter* where there were many tall trees amongst a great forest.

[father calls friend and they talk]

Calling his friend, the father explained what the family wanted. Yes, the family wanted to move to the wilderness for it's peacefulness, but at the same time they wanted the home to be available for their many friends from the city. These friends would surely want to visit. ((They wanted the road to their new home to remain woodsy, sort of like a pathway, but it must be straight enough for their city friends to find.))

[carpenter says yes, rents plane and surveys the area]

The *carpenter agreed and began to make plans.* If he was to prepare, clear and build this home, it was necessary to first choose the right location. *Renting an airplane,* the friend instructed the *pilot to fly* over an area that he was familiar with. "Oh yes, *he found* the right spot, down there in the middle of the forest, next to the beautiful meadow."

[carpenter gets equipment ready — then thinks]

After landing in great excitement, he quickly got his equipment together. Before beginning construction he took time to remember *the father's wishes that the road remain woodsy and straight.*

[bulldozer ready to go]

As the equipment moved in, the bulldozer carefully knocked down and removed some of the trees which blocked the pathway to where the home would be built. When the road was finished, the *carpenter looked back at it.* He could see it was sparsely cleared ((looked woodsy)) and straight but definitely a bit narrow. Nonetheless it was not hard to find if someone were REALLY looking, nor was it impossible to get to from the main road. ((I'm sure the carpenter was pleased that he'd accomplished what the father and his family had asked for. Now he could begin to build their home.))

[carpenter calls family]
[family listens to father talk]

The *carpenter immediately called* the father and told him the good news and how the building plans were coming. Once again *he reassured the family* that anyone REALLY looking for their home would surely find it.

The moral of this story is:

1. No matter how narrow or uncleared a road is, anyone REALLY looking for it will find it.

This has been a paraphrased scriptural drama according to God, Gail, Carol and kids.

FOLLOW-UP QUESTIONS

1. How do we prepare our road to God? (By talking with Him.)

2. God's way is often a narrow road. (Give an example)

SUMMARY STATEMENT

The road leading to the family's home would be slightly uncleared and a bit narrow, just as God's gate to everlasting life is narrow. Yes, it will be difficult to find, but all who REALLY look for it will find it.

We Really Looked and We Found

SURPRISED!

TITLE:	**SURPRISED**
SCRIPTURE:	Mark 12:10-11
	Good News/Jerusalem
THEME/REASON:	Seeing value and usefulness in all
KEY WORDS:	value, usefulness, surprised, judging
DRAMA TIME:	7-10 minutes
BY:	God, Gail, Carol and kids

As this drama unfolds, the cast will, by character, turn towards the audience and perform action to fit the italicized instructions. Use your own imagination to add or delete actions.

CAST:

parachute jumpers (as many as you can work with)
parachute maker
pilot
Jump Master
students to hold scenery

PHYSICAL PROPS:

1. Bible

2. Make-up (use to put a cross on cheek of each participant)

3. Large colorful banner depicting the theme

MIMED PROPS:

1. As discussed earlier, we are trying to simplify the use of physical props through the use of pantomime. When the cast cleans closets, boards the plane, jumps etc., exaggerated mime will emphasize the action.

2. Use any created activity that will add to the storyline.

• When writing the drama, frequently refer back to scripture, making sure you are saying the same thing only in today's words. You need to be scripturally accurate.

• Use the key words as a question-answer session after the drama. These key words will come in handy for reinforcement which will begin immediately after the drama and continue with follow-up a week later.

• Whenever a narrator's thought is to be interjected into the drama, it will be put in a set of double (())s.

To Begin:

NARRATOR: *enters* and tells audience to *"Pull Shades."*
CAST: *enters* and *turns back* to the audience.
NARRATOR: says *"Open Shades,"* then *proceeds* with the scripture reading, followed by the narration.

Narration:

The jumpers of Parachute Test Systems, China Lake, California, were in the process of *cleaning out their closets.* Out went all of the faded and slightly patched up parachutes.

[jumpers clean, parachute-maker tries to tell ...]

This was somewhat *upsetting to the gentleman* who made the parachutes. He kept *telling the jumpers,* "Just because the chutes don't look like your fancy new ones doesn't mean they can't be used. I know they are good and dependable."

[parachute maker hides his chute, jumpers clean]

No amount of talking would do, so out went all of the seemingly old and useless chutes. *Everything was discarded,* all but the one the *maker saved and hid,* ((for himself)) in the Buffalo ((this was the favorite of all planes to jump from)). He knew his creation better than anyone else and still felt it was able to do the job it was cut out for.

[all enter Buffalo, gaze from window as plane climbs]

One day the jumpers and the parachute maker were scheduled to jump from the Buffalo. *As the plane hit 16,000 feet* the engines began to gear down and all jumpers were *given the sign by the Jump Master* to leave the plane.

[maker last to jump, pilot flys to hangar]

All jumpers had brand spanking new Ram-Air Chutes. *Out they went free falling beautifully.* John the pilot, as *he flew back* to the hangar, noticed them in their famous *hand to hand circle pattern.*

[all land and watch parachute maker come in]

Unfortunately each of their chutes developed a small leak, which caused them to land in a sloppy way. The chutists all watched as the tattered and patched chute of the parachute maker brought him to a *perfect stand up landing*. ((Stand up landings are best, and can only be done with the finest parachute.))

[cast shows surprise as they lend an ear]

This chute, considered by the jumpers to be worthless, had become the most impressive and SURPRISING of all. The *parachutists were wonderfully SURPRISED* to see such worth in something they were ready to throw away.

The moral of this story is:

1. By throwing away certain tattered things, we may miss the most important, useful and well built of all.

2. Even though something may appear useless, we could be wonderfully SURPRISED.

This has been a paraphrased scriptural drama according to God, Gail, Carol and kids.

FOLLOW-UP QUESTIONS

1. Have you ever judged or turned someone away and to your surprise found that they had much to teach you? (ask for examples)

2. Who in the New Testament was rejected and thrown away by the people of the times?

SUMMARY STATEMENT

As the parachute maker tried over and over to tell the jumpers of the value and usefulness of the old chute, so too does God tell us of the value and usefulness of what seems to be the least of his people.

"We Value"
"Not Judge"

PROOF of the PUDDING

TITLE:	**PROOF OF THE PUDDING**
SCRIPTURE:	2 Corinthians 3:18
THEME/REASON:	A "Thank You" to Gail
KEY WORDS/IDEAS:	"You let me see God" "You Light Up My Life"
DRAMA TIME:	7 minutes
BY:	God, and 1982-83 7th and 8th grade class of St. Ann's School, Ridgecrest, CA.

BACKGROUND

After a year of writing and performing dramas with the students of St. Ann's, the one class that everyone said wouldn't be interested had actually been absorbing the drama messages and techniques all along.

Instead of writing a simple thank you card when Gail was preparing to move, they created and mimed a short drama. Their creation included a planned and practiced song and signs of the deaf.

Their drama was never meant to be polished or professional, merely a means of expressing their message, an answer to a need. The simplicity of their drama PROVES that anyone, with a desire, can create and adapt scripture.

To summarize "Proof Of The Pudding," the authors responded the way in which they were taught. Through Gail and the scripture-related dramas, they saw and experienced God's light on them, reflecting back through a drama of their own.

CAST:

God
Children of the school
Gail

PHYSICAL PROPS:

Bible
Podium (God looking over the world)

MIMED PROPS:

To keep it simple, the students used imagination to create physical and mimed props.

PROOF OF THE PUDDING

We were told that in "no way" would seventh and eighth-graders want to be involved in scriptural dramas. Well, before we knew it, they were wanting to be involved and asked us if they could help. Finally, as a "Thank You" to Gail, they wrote and performed their own drama. The following is the "Proof of the Pudding."

- "You Light Up My Life" — This song was performed with the use of sign language for the deaf.

To Begin:

NARRATOR: *enters* and *tells* audience to *"Pull Shades."*
CAST: *enters* and *turns back* to audience.
NARRATOR: says *"Open Shades,"* then *proceeds* with scripture reading, followed by narration.

Narration:

As God *looked over* his world one day, He *decided* to concentrate on Ridgecrest. *He said,* "There is a school with lovely children. With a little more guidance, why, they would SHINE!"

He *saw little children* playing prison ball and *smiled. Looking closer,* though, He saw that the *children threw the ball* extra hard at an unpopular child. The *smile disappeared.*

He heard children argue and use bad words. He even saw an occasional *fist fight.*

"With a little help," He thought, "these children could act a lot more Christian."

I need someone to reach out to the children. Someone that will really make a difference. — And then — *she came.* She *did dramas* and *made us think.* She reflected God's light and made us realize that his Word is for us too.

The moral of the story is that God within you lights up and transforms our life.

 And so, with lots of love we say THANKS to our friend Gail.

Song: "You Light Up My Life"

This has been a paraphrased scriptural drama according to God, and the seventh and eighth grade class.

SUMMARY STATEMENT

By reflecting God's glory, we and those around us will be transformed.

I LIKED YOUR DRAMAS BECAUSE...

helped us learn more about God.
Tony Carlon

helped me follow christ.
Paul Gage

made me think
Marvin Majors

made me think about God.
Cathy Gonder

light my life. Your dramas are good and show love respect for the school.
Sincerely,
Jimmy Koch

They are fun. From:
Jerri Hurst

help us be in a good mood
Tony Ulbrich

made me think
Erick O. Winter

CHECKLIST

CRITIQUES

REFLECTIONS

NOTES

JUST A REMINDER

PRE-DRAMA LIST

1. _____ Have you communicated with...
   _____ Leaders of group you are working with?
   _____ All members involved?
2. _____ Have you developed "Key Words"?
3. _____ Have you located through resource books, specific scripture quotes to give credibility to your message?
4. _____ Have you prayed, relaxed and digested the material at hand?
5. _____ Have you jotted down thoughts and impressions given to you by the Holy Spirit?
6. _____ Have you begun to write (drama, follow-up questions, summary, itemized checklist)?
7. _____ Have you edited your drama with a friend,(remembering to keep it simple)?

DAY OF DRAMA LIST

1. _____ Have you selected a place to practice and perform?
2. _____ Do you have props in hand or in mind?
3. _____ Do you have your cast chosen?
4. _____ Have you asked for mime suggestions from the children?
5. _____ Have you practiced briefly?
6. _____ Have you remembered to use simple make-up? (Invite the children to help paint each other.)
7. _____ Have you prayed with your cast?
8. _____ Are your narrator and cast set to go?
9. _____ Have you selected a song and or activity to reinforce the drama?
10. _____ If you are using any equipment today, is it ready?

POST DRAMA LIST

1. _____ Have you recapped the drama after the performance?
2. _____ Have you done a follow-up reinforcement a week later? (artwork and teacher critique)
3. _____ Have you displayed artwork and studied teacher critiques?

CRITIQUE SHEET

DRAMA TITLE: _____

DRAMA SCRIPTURE: _____

THEME/REASON: _____

DATE/TIME: _____

(Please mark the boxes with ...)

Y for yes, **N**, for no, or **S** for "somewhat"

1. **GOD'S WORD:**

   ☐ a. Did the drama relate to scripture in today's language?

2. **AUDIENCE:**

   ☐ a. Did the children (audience) come away with a "one liner"?

   ☐ b. Can everyone adapt the scripture reading to something specific in his or her life?

   ☐ c. Did the audience participate in the drama, song or activity you used to reinforce the message.

3. **CAST:**

   ☐ a. Did you observe a sense of pride, success and belief in what the cast was doing?

4. **FOLLOW-UP:**

   ☐ a. Were you able to pick up on two or three key words that you'll use as a follow-up this next week?

   ☐ b. Did it give you any ideas for reinforcement of scripture?

5. **SUCCESS:**

   ☐ a. Do you perceive it will make a difference to cast and audience alike?

6. **COMMENTS:**

   Please give any personal feelings, negative or positive, you had concerning this adapted scriptural drama.

QUIET THOUGHTS

QUIET THOUGHTS

In order for me to become at one with the Word of God, enough to adapt it to today, I must give God some alone time. I'd like to share a meditation that I experience with Him.

Finding a scripture that speaks to me in a special way is very important. It needs to be something that will carry me through the day. I have chosen to memorize Psalm 46:1-3 which deals with God being our "shelter" and our "strength".

REFLECTIONS

As I proceed through my "alone time with God" I ask Him...

1. How do you love me God? _____
2. How do you forgive me God? _____
3. How do you teach me God? _____
4. What is my purpose in life God? _____
5. Why do I meditate God? _____
6. Have I thanked you God? _____

MY OFFERING

I offer my day for _____ God, I know you will always be there to help. You will never tire of being my shelter and strength. I'm determined to make this meditation work for the glory of your name through my daily acts. I'm constantly trying to be patient for your time and not mine.

Let my affections towards my husband, children, and friends flow freely before they've lost interest, grown-up or moved away. I don't want their time with me to become a time of the past, but instead to remain with me always.

I must forgive with open arms and no gray sheet pulled down or it is not a true and real "forgive." A happy heart is the fruit of a true and real "forgive." Forgiveness happens with a Spirit and knowledge that the forgiver and forgivee has loved.

I know at times there is an evil spirit that creeps into my life. I neither want him nor do I turn him away. It is when my heart opens the door to Jesus, that I can spit upon the evil spirit (whozits) and crush his very being! At that point I hope to have learned and grown up in the Spirit of Goodness.

PERSONAL INTERCESSION

Help me Lord, especially in the following areas:

1. _____

2. _____

3. _____

Help me to thank you for these crosses, knowing they are instruments of personal growth.

Help me to offer my talents to your greater glory.

I must learn gentleness. I'm hoping the extrovert in me can allow a space to learn gentleness and the art of holding back when necessary. This gentleness help me to know and freely give my spouse, my children and friends the space they need to develop and grow in your light.

I will try Lord, to keep my thoughts on you so that I may see and recognize you today.

INTERCESSION FOR OTHERS

Please call _____ by name Lord. I want _____ to know and experience what being loved by you can mean. What an intimate relationship with you can do for his/her life.

Please bring _____ to You Lord. Let him/her be touched by your Spirit so he/she may in turn bring others to you. He/She has so much love to give, let it be given in YOUR NAME. For you are greater than all of us, none of us could have created any of these worldly marvels, without first being touched by your supreme love and power and knowledge.

Lord I pray for my government and it's leaders. Mostly about wars and nuclear war.

I pray about the communist ruled countries and their leaders as well as our own. Holy Spirit help us to see more clearly. Help us make decisions for the good of all.

Nuclear War is an end to an end. Please Lord, take this burden away and grant world leaders the power to see good in control and restraint.

We Americans are not perfect, but the freedom we have is quite like a good meal, savor it and appreciate it. Don't let anyone dishonor it or the chef.

* * *

The giver or volunteer is only a channel for the gifts received from God. One cannot hoard or withhold them without blocking the channel. A true volunteer gives of self not for self glory and pride but to share in the gifts, to become a channel for God's love so that all may be touched and see the "Face of Jesus."

* * *

Thank you Lord for being who you are and accepting me for who I am.

You are my Greatest Example and Lover. Powerful!

NOTES